1 Pinch of Sunshine, ½ Cup of Rain

Natural Food Recipes For Young People

Ruth Cavin

Illustrated by Frances Gruse Scott

ATHENEUM 1973 NEW YORK

To Frances Goldin,
whose deep concern
for the way children grow
has led to this book

Text copyright © 1973 by Ruth Cavin
Illustrations copyright © 1973 by Frances Gruse Scott
All rights reserved
Library of Congress catalog card number 72-86928
ISBN 0-689-30099-9
Published simultaneously in Canada by
McClelland & Stewart, Ltd.
Manufactured in the United States of America
Printed by Connecticut Printers, Inc.
Hartford, Connecticut
Bound by A. Horowitz & Son/Bookbinders
Clifton, New Jersey
First Edition

Contents

What It's All About

When you're very little, you make things like mud pies and soapsud soup. When you get bigger, you want to cook foods that people really can eat (and you like to hear them ask, "Did *you* make this? It's good!").

Here's a cookbook with recipes for good-tasting dishes using foods that are as wholesome and natural as the sun and rain that made them.

There are snacks you'll be able to gobble without hearing anyone say, "I *wish* you wouldn't fill up on that junk!" There are vegetable dishes that are as much fun to eat as to make. You'll meet old favorites like pizza and Sloppy Joes, and new tastes to surprise your family with.

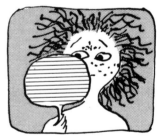

Every recipe has been chosen for easy cooking, happy eating . . . and shining good health. These foods make you strong, not fat. After eating whole grains and proteins, fresh fruits and vegetables, you'll find you're getting fewer colds and stomach-aches. Your dentist may have less drilling and filling to do. You'll have bright eyes and clear skin, and you'll feel more alive!

Best of all, natural foods *taste* so good! Especially when you've cooked them yourself!

Safe at Home!

Read these rules over again every time you cook until you know them all by heart!

1. Tie back long hair before starting to work. Wash your hands.
2. Cook on the back burners, and turn long handles toward the back.
3. If your oven must be lit with a match, be sure you know the safe way to do it.
4. Never pour hot grease into water; it spits.
5. Never pour water into hot grease; it spits.

6. Before taking anything from the stove, be sure you have a heatproof place to put it. (You'll look pretty silly running around waving a hot pan!)

7. Wipe up all spills right away. Kitchen floors, like roads, are slippery when wet.

8. Tilt the lid of a hot pot or pan away from you when taking it off to keep from being burned by hot steam.

9. Know where the baking soda is and how to use it on a grease fire. Never throw water on burning grease!

It's Time To Cook

Choose your recipe and *read it all the way through!* This is very important and prevents unpleasant surprises. It is a bit embarrassing to half mix a cake and then find you haven't the ingredients to finish it.

Check the kitchen for what you need. If you haven't got everything, go out and buy what's missing, or figure out a substitute (you may need help), or borrow it . . . or decide to cook something else!

Almost all the ingredients called for in this book can be found at any grocery or super-market. A few will have to be bought at a health-food store or in the health-food depart-ment of some regular store. Those foods are marked in the recipes with an asterisk. Some-times a food is marked because a special form of it can be found in health-food stores. For instance, coconut is everywhere, but *unsweet-ened* coconut is special. If you can't get the special kind, use what you can.

Lay out all the ingredients in an orderly way. Then get out the tools you will need: measuring cups and spoons, mixing spoons, bowls and so on. You'll be surprised how much easier cook-ing is if you do all these things first.

And when you've finished . . . don't leave a trace!

Tell yourself that Sherlock Holmes or Perry Mason or Ironside is coming to your house to look for a clue that someone has been using the kitchen. Foil him by leaving it just the way it was when you started to cook.

Take care of things as you go along. When you use an ingredient, cover the container and set it to one side, out of the way. Whenever possible, put used dishes in the sink, filled with water.

At cleaning-up time, wipe drips and finger marks from the containers of food with a damp cloth or sponge and put them away. Wash, dry and put away all dishes or load them into the dishwasher. Wipe counters and tabletops and the handles of drawers and the refrigerator. Sweep the floor.

That Super Snooper mustn't suspect you've even *been* there!

A CLUE!

CHAPTER 1

Top Of The Morning To You!

It's called "break-fast" because you really break a fast when you eat it. Overnight is the longest between-meal stretch in our day. To get a head start on your morning, eat a breakfast that gives you what you need—energy!

Fruit

One of America's best food habits is taking fruit or fruit juice first thing in the morning. The fresh taste wakes up your mouth. The vitamin C in fruit builds and repairs bones and teeth, our smallest blood vessels, and the "cement" between our body cells. This is the vitamin that helps us fight off colds and other infections.

All fruit has some vitamin C. Citrus fruits— oranges, grapefruit, tangerines—have a lot. So do tomatoes. Use fresh-squeezed or unsweetened frozen orange juice, and don't squeeze or mix it until you're ready to drink it.

Good as orange juice is, changing to something else now and then makes mornings more interesting. In the summer, there's a rainbow of fresh fruit to choose from: peaches, plums, grapes, apricots, berries, cherries, pears or melons. Rinse it all well, shake it dry, and pile it into a big bowl for everyone to take.

Or slice one or two kinds of fruit into saucers. (Don't slice little things like raspberries or cherries, silly! Use your head!)

If you hate peach fuzz, rub it off with a clean towel. Or peel the peach, if you must!

to peel a peach

Fill a saucepan about 2/3 full of water and put it over high heat. When it boils (see page 92), pick up a washed peach on the end of a long fork and dip it into the water. Count slowly to eleven (or some number near it—ten, perhaps, or twelve). Then take it out, hold it under running cold water and count three. You'll find you can pull the skin right off.

Melons get sliced the long way in 2 – or 4 – or 8. Scoop out the seeds. Give each person a slice of melon on a plate and a piece of lemon or lime to squeeze over it.

Or cut the seeded melon into little crescents. Arrange them in a swirl on a platter and let people eat them with their hands.

For a special breakfast, get 2 or more different kinds of melon. With a ball cutter, make little melon balls. Use an emptied half melon as a serving bowl. (Save the extra bits for a melon cup the next day. Keep them in the refrigerator, covered.)

Nothing is more delicious than A Big Bowl of Berries. Get more than one kind if you can,

rinse them all with cold water, shake dry and mix them. Use strawberries, huckleberries, raspberries, blackberries . . . maybe some grow where you can pick them, before the birds do!

A fruit North Americans are discovering is the tropical mango. It's one of the oldest fruits known, and one of the best. A mango tastes something like a peach, something like a melon, and something like the way fruit must taste in Heaven!

To eat a mango, cut 4 slits in the skin from top to bottom. Take hold of the top of each section and pull it down and off. Slice the fruit away from the pit, which is large and flat. The slicer gets to chew the pit and pull the extra fruit off with his teeth!

In winter there is still fresh fruit—citrus from Florida, California and Texas; bananas and pineapples from Mexico, Hawaii and Central America.

Tropical Winter Bowl

(4 servings)

2 navel oranges
1 grapefruit
1 ripe pineapple (ask at the store if it's ripe)
1 banana
½ cup shredded coconut (if you like)
   Try to get the unsweetened* kind.

(Pineapples take time to clean. Skip the pineapple if you want to. Or do it the evening before and store the pieces, covered, in the refrigerator.)

Slice the end off an orange or grapefruit. Use your fingers to pull off the skin. Do this over a bowl, as it is a drippy operation and you want to save the juice.

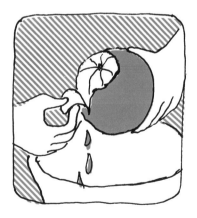

Put the peeled fruit on a plate and cut it in half across the sections. Pull the pieces apart and drop them in with the juice.

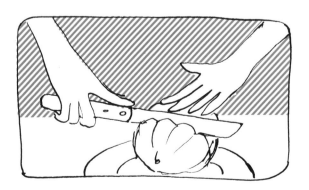

If you *do* use a pineapple, cut off the leafy top with a big sharp knife. (You'll get some pineapple with it. Don't worry.)

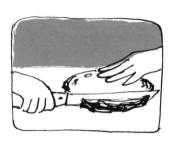

Stand the fruit on its bottom and carefully cut it right down the middle from top to bottom. Cut each half into thick slices. With a smaller knife, peel off the rind from each slice. Cut each piece into smaller pieces. Slice off the point of each—that's the core. Put the pineapple in with the other fruit.

Peel the banana and cut it into round slices. (Don't do this ahead of time; the air will darken a naked banana.) Add it to the other fruit and mix it well. Sprinkle coconut over the top (if you're using it).

Cooked Dried Fruit

Prunes, raisins, currants, figs and dates are in every grocery. Your store probably sells dried peaches, pears and apples, too. Dried fruits are sweeter than fresh; they're little bombs of energy—with some vitamins and minerals, too. Their sugar is natural, not refined, but it can cause cavities just as candy does. So brush your teeth after you eat dried fruit—or at least swish a mouthful of water around *very* hard!

> 2 cups of any dried fruit or a combination
> of several kinds
> 1 cup of water or apple cider

Rinse the fruit in cold water. Put it in a saucepan and just cover it with water or cider. (Cider makes a sweeter dish.) Cook it over medium heat until the liquid starts to boil (see page 92). Then turn the heat to low, and let the fruit simmer (see page 92) for 10 minutes.

Eat cooked dried fruit plain, over cooked or dry cereal, or over ice cream.

Oatmeal Plus

(4 servings)

Here's a good breakfast all in one bowl that will keep you going in high gear all morning long.

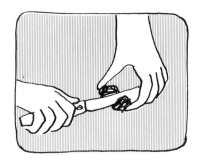

1½ cups oatmeal. "Quick-cooking" or "old-fashioned," but not "instant."
2 Tablespoons toasted wheat germ
3 cups skim or whole milk
¾ teaspoon salt
½ cup any kind of dried fruit
a big shake of powdered cinnamon

If the fruit is in big pieces, cut it into small pieces. Measure the oatmeal into a bowl and add the wheat germ to it.

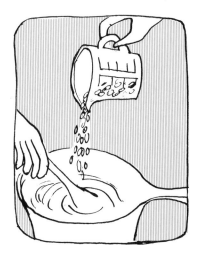

Measure the milk into a saucepan. Add the salt and dried fruit. Heat it over medium heat until little bubbles start coming up around the edges.

Add the oatmeal slowly, stirring all the while. Stir for a minute or two after the oatmeal is all in, and then let it cook. If it bubbles very fast, turn the heat down. Stir it once or twice every few minutes. Cook it from 3 to 8 minutes, depending on how thick you like it.

Eat the oatmeal (in England it's called "porridge!") with milk and a sprinkle of cinnamon over the top. Spoon some honey or brown sugar over it—you won't need much, because the fruit sweetens it.

Luscious Mush

(4 servings)

I don't know why this good cereal has such a messy name. The Pilgrims called it "samp." Is that better or worse?

    4 cups water
    1 cup cornmeal (stone ground* is best)
    1 teaspoon salt

Put 3 cups of the water and the salt in a saucepan and bring it to a boil over medium heat.

Mix the cornmeal with 1 cup of cold water. When the water in the saucepan boils, add the wet cornmeal. Stir it as you do, and keep stirring until it gets thick—about 1 minute.

Turn the heat to very low, and cook until the mush is quite thick. The bubbles come up to the top and look like tiny volcanoes as they break. It will take 2 or 3 minutes at the most. Stir often.

Serve the mush with molasses and milk, or use maple syrup.

If any is left over, put it in a pan and keep it in the refrigerator. The next day, slice it and fry it in corn oil margarine. Serve with maple syrup or some other topping.

Morning Mixups

Almost everyone likes "dry" cereal in the morning—cereal that you don't have to cook, but can just pour milk over and eat. Here is a recipe for a very special kind. It's full of flavor, loaded with food value, and it even has a history!

It was invented about a hundred years ago by a Swiss doctor named Bircher-Brenner. The people of Switzerland have been eating it almost by the *ton* ever since! They have it for breakfast, as a lunch dish, even instead of soup at dinner!

It's called "Bircher Meusli," which means "Bircher's Porridge."

After you've made Bircher Meusli, there is a recipe for mixing your own personal dry cereal that you make up yourself. You can name it after yourself—"Debbie-Bits" or "Ron's Rumbles" or "Darlinis." Think of something to go with your own name.

Decorate an empty coffee can as your cereal package. (Will you give a "free offer" on the back?) Maybe you'll become famous for your cereal, the way Dr. Bircher-Brenner did.

Bircher Meusli (2 servings)

1/3 cup uncooked oatmeal (Use "quick-cooking," not "instant" nor old-fashioned.")*

3 Tablespoons water

2 Tablespoons lemon juice

2 apples

2 Tablespoons honey

¼ cup nuts

Mix the oatmeal and water and set it aside. Squeeze the lemon, measure 2 Tablespoons of juice.

Wash the apples. Cut them in 4 down the middle and cut away the core. On a grater, grate the apples into the lemon juice. Try to grate some of the peel in too.

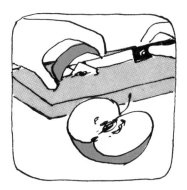

Add the honey to the apple-lemon mixture. (Hold the spoon under hot water first, so the honey will slide off. Use your finger to push off the last bit. Then lick your finger!)

Put the nuts in the blender, turn it on, count five, turn it off. If you have no blender, use a chopping jar or cut the nuts with a knife.

Mix everything together. Eat it with milk.

Change-arounds: Use another kind of fruit, cut up or grated.

Use whole-wheat flakes* or millet flakes* instead of part of the oatmeal.

Made-To-Order Mixup (a big batch)

Choose one kind or more from each group:

Cereal: 1½ cups any kind of whole grain flakes. There are wheat,* buckwheat,* millet,* barley,* soya,* oatmeal and more.

Fruit: 1 cup any kind: raisins, apricots, pitted prunes, dates, peaches, figs, pears.

Nuts And Things: ½ cup chopped nuts (chop in the blender or with a knife or chopping jar), unsweetened shredded coconut,* hulled pumpkin, or sunflower seeds, sesame seeds, little pine nuts (pignolias).

Cut the dried fruit into small bits with a kitchen shears dipped in hot water.

Mix everything together in a big bowl, and put it in a jar with a lid for storage. When you're ready to eat it, sprinkle

1 Tablespoon wheat germ

on each serving. Pour milk over it, or mix it with plain yogurt.

If you like it sweeter, add 1 Tablespoon of honey, maple syrup or molasses to each serving.

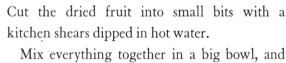

Change-around: Rub ¼ cup of brown sugar through a strainer and mix it with the dry ingredients instead of using honey or syrup.

Eggs

Inside the brown or white shell of an egg there is a small magic: a delicious food that is easy to cook any one of a number of ways, that doesn't cost much, isn't fattening, and is loaded with protein, iron, and vitamin D—all in one neat little package.

"Egg," said a scientist who had spent years studying this interesting food, "is all."

Scrambled With Skill (2 servings)

Get everything else ready before you begin to cook the eggs. The best scrambled eggs are cooked *very* slowly. Use a small, heavy pan:

> 4 eggs
> 1 Tablespoon milk
> about ½ teaspoon corn oil margarine

Break the eggs into a bowl. Add the milk and beat the mixture with a fork or wire whisk until there are little bunches of bubbles on the top.

Put the pan over low heat. Let it heat up for a minute and then add the margarine. Tilt the pan to help it spread as it melts.

Pour in the eggs and stir them with a spoon as they cook. Stop for a minute or two, then stir again. Keep doing this until the eggs are solid, but still a little wet. Sprinkle with a little salt and ground black pepper and serve.

> Change-arounds: Beat 2 Tablespoons of cottage cheese into the eggs before you cook them.
>
> OR add ½ cup grated yellow cheese.

Coddled With Care (2 servings)

Have you ever heard of "coddled" eggs? If not, have you heard of "soft-boiled" eggs? (Silly question!) "Coddling" means treating very gently. Eggs come out better that way than if they are actually boiled.

If you follow this recipe, you won't have to guess about the time:

> 4 eggs
> 1 Tablespoon salt
> cold water

Put the eggs into an enamel or stainless steel saucepan. (Eggshells darken aluminum pans.) Add the salt and cover the eggs with cold water.

Put the pan over low heat and when the water boils, turn off the heat. With a slotted spoon take out each egg and hold it under running cold water. Serve the eggs in egg cups or saucers, and let everyone open his own.

This makes an egg that is as "done" as a 3-minute boiled egg. If you like yours cooked more, turn off the heat when the water boils, but let the eggs sit in the pan for 1 more minute.

Pancakes : How We Bake Them

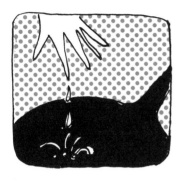

Although pancakes are made on a pan or a griddle, they are not fried—they're baked. You use just enough fat to keep them from sticking. Heavy pans or griddles work best for baking them, and the old-fashioned iron ones are best of all.

Get everything else ready before you start to bake the pancakes. Put the pan or griddle over high heat. Let it get hot for 2 or 3 minutes. Shake a wet finger at it. If the drops of water sizzle, and do a little skip before disappearing, the pan is hot enough.

Turn the heat down a little and melt just enough corn oil margarine in the pan to cover the bottom. (Spread it with a spoon or spatula.)

Dip big spoonfuls of batter onto the pan. Leave enough space so the cakes can spread. If

they do run together, just cut them apart. After about 1 minute, bubbles will start showing at the top of the cakes. Turn them over and bake them on the other side for about 1 more minute. (Lift the edge and peer under to see if it is brown enough.)

If the margarine smokes, the pan is too hot. Turn down the heat a bit.

Whole Wheat Pancakes

(Makes 12 large ones)

1½ cups whole wheat flour
3 Tablespoons brown sugar
1 teaspoon salt
3 teaspoons baking powder
2 eggs
1¼ cups milk
3 Tablespoons corn oil
corn oil margarine for greasing the griddle

Mix the flour, sugar, salt and baking powder in a bowl. In another bowl, break the eggs and add the milk and the oil to them.

Beat the liquid mixture just enough to mix it together.

Make a dent in the middle of the dry ingredients with your hand or a spoon and pour the liquid into this little well. Stir it quickly until it is mixed. Never mind the lumps.

Bake the cakes as it tells you on the page before this.

Johnnycakes

Some people say these were first called "journeycakes," because the early settlers, going on a trip, would take a great big corn cake in their saddlebag to eat on the way.

2 cups buttermilk
½ cup rye flour* (or whole wheat or unbleached white flour)
2 large eggs
1 teaspoon baking soda
1 cup cornmeal (stone ground* or regular)
1 teaspoon salt

Put all these ingredients into a bowl, in the order named. Beat everything together until it is very well mixed. Bake the cakes as it tells you on the page before this.

Pancake Top-Offs

Sweet toppings that use natural sugar—more food value and easier on the teeth!

—Honey or maple syrup

—Fruit top: washed fresh small fruit (blueberries are wonderful). Sliced fruit, like peaches or bananas. Or a pleasant mush made from fresh or frozen fruit in the blender or with a potato masher.

—Triple dip: one teaspoonful of molasses, a squeeze of lemon juice, a small pat of butter or margarine.

—Homemade or bought applesauce with a sprinkle of cinnamon.

Recipes:

—Honey syrup

Mix 1/3 cup honey with 2 Tablespoons butter and ¼ cup water. Heat.

—Brown sugar syrup

Mix ¾ cup brown sugar with ¼ cup water in a saucepan. Heat, stirring to melt the sugar, until it starts to boil.

—Honey-orange syrup

Mix ¼ cup honey with ½ cup orange juice, a pat of butter and a nice hard squeeze of lemon juice. Heat it until it is very hot.

—Honey cream

Mix honey half-and-half with commercial sour cream or plain yogurt. Beat it until it is nice and fluffy.

Minute Milkshakes

It's late! It's late! There's no time for waffles and eggs and bacon and cereal and toast! It's too late!

That's no reason to skip breakfast. Not when you can make these delectable all-in-one concoctions with a whirl of the blender or a few good hard shakes of a jar.

Minute milkshakes are made from fruit, eggs and milk. And a dash of ice cream, if there's some in the freezer. It's very easy in a blender, and you have a wide choice of fresh and frozen fruit.

Blender Milkshakes (1 serving)

1 cup whole or skim milk

½ cup (about ¼ package) frozen fruit or
berries, melon, banana, peach or plum

1 egg (look it over carefully to be sure there
are no cracks in the shell)

1 scoop of ice cream, if you have it (If you
do, use only ¾ cup of milk.)

Wash fresh fruit and peel it if necessary.
Break frozen fruit up into small pieces. Put
everything into the blender. Cover and blend
for half a minute (while you count 30 slowly).
Pour into a big glass and have breakfast!

Change-arounds: Use buttermilk or plain
yogurt instead of milk. With it, add 1
Tablespoon honey, a sprinkle of salt, and
one of ground nutmeg.

OR Put in 1 Tablespoon wheat germ.

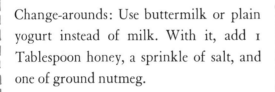

Vegetable Nog

1 cup tomato juice

1 egg

1 stalk celery

1 sprig parsley

1 strip green pepper

1 thin slice onion

Wash the vegetables and cut into pieces. Put
everything in the blender and blend for 1
minute, or until all the vegetables have dis-
appeared.

Change-around: Put some strips of washed carrot in it, too. Leave out the onion.

Cranberry Bog Nog (1 serving)

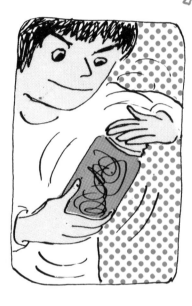

You can make this in a jar if you have no blender.

½ cup cranberry juice

½ cup plain yogurt

1 egg

1 teaspoon honey

Get a tall glass ready with 2 or 3 ice cubes in it.

Put everything else—cranberry juice, yogurt, egg and honey—into the blender or into a jar. Whirl the blender while you count 20, or count 20 while you shake the jar very hard.

Pour over ice and drink it with a straw.

Birthday Nog (1 serving)

½ cup milk

1 egg

½ cup fruit

2 scoops of the birthday person's favorite ice cream

Put all the ingredients except 1 scoop of ice cream into the blender. Blend while you count 30. Pour into a glass, float the other scoop of ice cream on top. Serve with a straw, a spoon, and a "Happy Birthday!"

CHAPTER 2

Soup And Some Sandwiches

In the Middle Ages, soup and bread were all that some of the poorer people had to eat. All the food that came their way went into a big pot that was kept simmering on the fire all day. When anyone was hungry, he dipped out a bowlful.

Many soups start with "stock"—a meat or chicken broth that takes time to make. You can use canned broth or "consomme" for your soup.

Here are three very different ones. Add one of the sandwiches, made with tasty whole grain bread, and you couldn't have a better lunch!

Golden Velvet Soup

(4 servings)

½ onion

1 Tablespoon corn oil margarine

6 carrots

1 cup or more of water

¼ cup orange juice

1½ cups chicken broth

3 Tablespoons canned tomato sauce

Peel the onion and cut it into very small pieces. Put them in a saucepan with the margarine over medium heat, and cook until the onion is yellow. Stir it from time to time.

Scrub the carrots and cut them into very thin slices. Add them and the water to the pan, and let the mixture cook slowly for a half hour, or until the carrots are very soft. Add more water if you need it.

Put the carrots and the liquid they were cooked in into the blender. (Or push them with their liquid through a sieve.) Add the orange juice. Blend for 1½ minutes, until the mixture is smooth. (If you've sieved the carrots, mix them well with the orange juice.)

Put the carrots back in the pan, add the broth and tomato sauce, and heat over low heat. Serve when it is hot.

Egg Drop Soup

... and you really do *drop* in the eggs!

(4 servings)

2 cans (about 3 cups) chicken broth
2 eggs
1/4 teaspoon salt

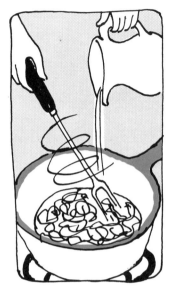

Put the soup in a saucepan over medium high heat. Be sure the pan is large enough to allow the soup room to boil busily.

While the soup heats, break the eggs into a bowl and add the salt. Whip them with a fork or a wire whisk until they are bubbly and mixed well. Pour them into a pitcher.

When the soup is boiling very fast, slowly pour the eggs into it. As you do, beat them into the soup with a long-handled cooking fork. The hot soup will cook the eggs into lacylike strings. As soon as the eggs are all in, the soup is ready to eat.

Down East Fish Chowder

(4 servings)

Some say chowder is not a soup, it's a stew. Make this and see which side you're on.

2 medium-sized potatoes
1 onion
1 teaspoon salt
3 Tablespoons parsley
1 pound filet of sole or flounder, fresh or frozen
2 cups milk
another teaspoon salt
1/4 teaspoon pepper

If the fish is frozen, let it thaw enough so that you can separate the pieces and cut them up.

Peel the potatoes and cut them into small cubes. Peel the papery skin from the onion and slice it. Put both vegetables into a saucepan with 1 teaspoon of the salt and enough water to cover them. Bring this to a boil over high heat, lower the heat to medium, let it cook for 10 minutes. The vegetables will be just not quite as soft as we usually eat them.

Run cold water over the parsley, and use kitchen shears to cut it into small pieces.

Cut the fish into pieces about 2 inches square and add it to the vegetables. Cook 5 minutes more.

Put the milk in another pan and heat it until little bubbles form around the edges. Pour it into the fish and vegetable mixture. Taste it for salt and pepper, add more if necessary.

Serve the chowder very hot sprinkled with chopped parsley.

Some sandwich spreads

Handmade Peanut Butter

(for a peanut-butter-and-honey sandwich)

   1 cup peanuts in the shell
   2 Tablespoons corn or peanut oil
   ¾ teaspoon salt

Shell the peanuts. Grind them, a few at a time, in a food grinder. Use the finest blade—the one with no holes in it.

Mix the oil and salt into the ground nuts.

Store what you don't use in the refrigerator. A sandwich: Spread whole wheat bread with peanut butter. Put honey on that, and another slice of whole wheat bread. A sandwich!

Change-around: Make *cashew*-nut butter!

Banapple Spread

For 2 sandwiches:

   1 banana
   1 apple
   1 squeeze lemon juice

Peel and core the apple. Put both fruits in the blender, cut in pieces. Blend 30 seconds.

OR Grate the apple; mash the banana with a fork.

Mix the two fruits and squeeze lemon juice over them. Spread on some interesting dark bread, like dark pumpernickel or rye.

Sea Devils (2 sandwiches or 2 deviled eggs)

2 eggs
1 small can tuna (3½ ounces)
1 teaspoon prepared mustard
2 shakes of paprika
salt if you need it

Put the eggs in cold water in a small saucepan and bring to a boil over medium heat. Turn the heat down so the water just bubbles and cook, covered, for 12 minutes.

Run cold water over the eggs and take off the shells. Cut them in half around the middle. Mash the yolks with the tuna and mustard, using a fork, or blend them in the blender. Add the paprika, taste to see whether to add salt.

Fill the whites with the mixture. Cut the filled eggs in slices for sandwiches—or eat them as is!

Crunch Lunch

For each sandwich:

1 medium-sized carrot
1 Tablespoon plain yogurt
¼ teaspoon salt

Scrub the carrot and grate it. Use the middle-sized teeth of the grater. Mix the grated carrot with the yogurt and salt. Spread it on rye or whole wheat bread.

Chicken Liver Sandwich Spread

Make this the day before for a very special picnic. This makes 2 big sandwiches.

1 chicken liver
1 onion
1 egg
2 Tablespoons corn oil margarine
salt and pepper

Put the egg in a small steel or enamel saucepan with water to cover and ½ teaspoon salt. Bring to a boil over medium-low heat, turn the heat down and let it bubble slowly for 12 minutes. Take it from the pan, run cold water over it, and shell it.

Peel the onion, slice it into thin slices, then into bits. Cook it in margarine over medium heat until it is yellow brown.

When the egg is done, rinse the saucepan and put 1 cup of water and 1 teaspoon salt into it. Put it over the heat, and when the water boils, add the liver and cook it for 5 minutes.

Push the egg through a strainer. Cut the liver into tiny bits. Mash everything with a fork until well mixed. Add ½ teaspoon salt and a sprinkle of pepper. Spread slices of seeded rye bread or pumpernickel with the mixture.

Raisin Studded Cottage Cheese

For each sandwich, mix
  ¼ cup cottage cheese
  ¼ cup raisins

Spread on whole wheat bread.

CHAPTER 3

The Middle Of The Meal

When we ask "What's for dinner?" we don't expect to be told "salad" or "baked potatoes" or "grapefruit." What we mean is, what's the main course—the "star attraction?"

The main part of almost every meal is the protein food—meat, fish, poultry, eggs, milk or cheese. (Beans, lentils and some cereals have a bit of protein, too.) These are the foods we need for building new cells in our bodies, and for repairing damaged or worn cells.

When you make a main course, you can really say you've made the meal, even if someone else helps out with vegetables and dessert.

Hamburgers (4 servings)

Is there anyone who doesn't like hamburgers? They're easy to make, easy to serve, and *very* easy to eat!

4 slices whole wheat or rye bread

½ onion

1 pound chopped beef: chuck, round or sirloin. The better the meat is, the less fat it has to cook out and make your hamburgers shrink.

3 Tablespoons toasted wheat germ

1 "pinch" of marjoram (as much as you can pinch between your finger and thumb)

With a cookie cutter or the edge of a glass, cut circles in the bread so that you have 4 round slices. (If you make your hamburgers very skinny, you'll need more slices of bread.)

Peel the half onion and grate it into a bowl. With a fork, lightly mix the meat and wheat germ with the onion.

Put a heavy frying pan over medium heat. Wet your hands with cold water and make patties from the meat. Make thick patties or thin patties—however your family likes them. Put them on the hot pan.

Turn them after 2 minutes if they are very flat, after 4 minutes if they are very round. Cook them just as long on the second side. Sprinkle the done side with salt and marjoram.

If a lot of fat comes leaking out of the hamburgers as they cook, take them from the pan, put them on a plate, and pour the fat from the pan. Put the burgers back in.

While the meat cooks, toast the bread.

Cut into the thickest hamburger to see if it is the way you like it. If it is too red, cook longer.

Put a hamburger on each piece of toast, season the second side with salt and marjoram, and serve.

What Else? A lot of raw vegetables, with a dip sauce.

Change-around: Scrub a medium-sized carrot, grate, and add it to the meat mixture before you cook it.

Sloppy Joes

(4 servings)

Even easier than hamburgers!

1 pound chopped beef: chuck, round or sirloin

1 onion

1 green pepper

2 stalks celery

2 Tablespoons corn oil margarine

2 Tablespoons toasted wheat germ

1½ teaspoons salt

½ teaspoon pepper

1 12-ounce can tomato sauce

¼ teaspoon nutmeg or ½ teaspoon chili powder

6 slices whole wheat or rye bread

Clean the vegetables and cut them into little bits. Cook them, stirring often, in the margarine over medium high heat until they're soft.

Mix the meat and the wheat germ.

Take the vegetables from the pan and, in the same pan, stir the meat over medium high heat until it turns brown. Use a slotted spoon to take it out.

Pour the fat from the pan and put all the cooked ingredients back in, along with the salt, pepper and tomato sauce. Choose which spice you want to use; you might try one this time and the other the next. Add it.

Cover the pan and let the mixture cook 10 minutes. Toast the bread, cut each slice in 4 diagonally, and put the triangles around each pile of meat so it won't be *quite* so *sloppy!*

Veal Bits

(4 servings)

Veal is a particularly good meat to make if you're a beginner. It cooks quickly, and gives you a lot of protein for a little work.

> 1½ pounds veal scallopini (flat, boneless pieces of veal)
> 1 Tablespoon corn or olive oil
> 1 bay leaf
> ½ cup meat stock or consomme
> 3 Tablespoons lemon juice
> 1 teaspoon salt (or more or less, to taste)
> ¼ teaspoon paprika
> 1 big pinch of rosemary or ginger

Cut the veal into pieces about as wide as your little finger and half as long. Squeeze the lemon to make the lemon juice.

Put the oil in a heavy flat pan over medium heat, and heat it for 3 minutes. Then add the meat and the bay leaf. Stir the veal with a wooden spoon until it is a lovely golden color. This will take about 12 to 15 minutes. You'll find that there's a lot of liquid at first, but that in about 8 or 10 minutes this cooks away and the meat browns.

Smell the ginger (which is hot) and the rosemary (which is not), and decide which you want to use. Put it in. Add the stock or consomme and then the lemon juice. Add the salt and pepper, lower the heat, and let the veal cook for 5 more minutes.

What Else? This is good served over rice or noodles. Peas go well, too.

Great-Aunt Annie's Great Meat Balls (4 servings)

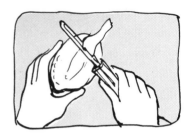

There are Swedish meatballs and Italian meatballs and meatballs that are people who do something dumb, and then there are my Great-Aunt Annie's meatballs. She made them every third Saturday night, when the whole family gathered at her house; and when someone had a birthday around that time, she would put a tiny prize in one meatball and make sure the birthday person got it.

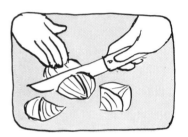

You learned to chew carefully when it was around your birthday!

See if you don't think Great-Aunt Annie's Great Meatballs are great!

> 1½ pounds ground beef (chuck, round or sirloin)
> The peel of ½ lemon
> 1½ big carrots
> 1½ big onions
> 1/3 cup meat stock, vegetable water, or plain water
> 3 Tablespoons toasted wheat germ
> 1½ Tablespoons ketchup
> 1½ teaspoons prepared mustard
> 1½ Tablespoons corn oil margarine
> 1½ teaspoons salt
> ½ teaspoon pepper
> ½ teaspoon powdered ginger

Use a vegetable scraper or a zester to take thin strips of peel from a washed lemon. Peel the onions and cut them into chunks. Wash the carrots and cut them into 1-inch pieces. Put the lemon peel, onions, carrots and 1/3 cup liquid into the blender, and whirl it for 1 whole minute.

If you have no blender, cut up the onions and the carrots, and the peel very fine.

Put everything together but the garlic and ginger and mix well with your hands. Make the meat into balls by tossing a handful gently back and forth from one hand to the other. Put the meatballs into a large pot that has a lid. Set it over low heat.

When juice and fat melt out around the meatballs, raise the heat to medium. Add the ginger to the pot.

Cover the pot and let the meatballs cook for 30 minutes. Every 5 minutes or so, give the pot a shake, to keep the meat from sticking to the bottom.

What Else? Baked potatoes and sliced cucumbers are easy to get ready.

Chicken Gizzard And Brown Rice Casserole

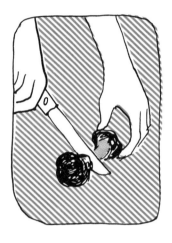

(4 servings)

"Gizzard" is a funny-sounding word. It makes me think about the man who went into a butcher shop and said, "Give me a pound of kiddleys, please."

"You mean 'kidneys,' don't you?" asked the butcher.

"I said 'kiddleys,' diddle I?" replied the man.

> 1 onion
> 3 Tablespoons corn oil margarine
> 1¼ pounds chicken gizzards
> 1/3 cup toasted wheat germ
> 1 Tablespoon salt
> 1 Tablespoon poultry seasoning
> ¼ teaspoon each marjoram and thyme
> 3 cups chicken broth (or 1 can of broth and 1 of water, or 3 cups of water and 4 chicken bouillon cubes).
> 1 cup brown rice

Peel the onion, slice it thin, and cut the slices into small bits. Put them in a frying pan with 1 Tablespoon of the margarine and cook them over medium low heat until they are golden yellow.

Light the oven and set it for 350°.

Clean the gizzards. Rinse them quickly in cold water and cut out the tough muscle between the 2 halves.

Mix the salt, poultry seasoning, marjoram, thyme and wheat germ. Roll the gizzards in this mixture.

Take the cooked onion from the pan and put it into a casserole. Add 2 more Tablespoons margarine to the pan and brown the gizzards over medium high heat, stirring them every few minutes. They will brown in about 5 to 7 minutes.

Put the browned gizzards into the casserole with the onion and the rice. Pour as much of the chicken broth or other liquid as fits comfortably into the frying pan. Heat it until it bubbles, and stir it with a fork to get all the good flavoring from the pan. Pour it into the casserole, and add the rest of the liquid, if any.

Cover the casserole and bake it in the oven for about 1 hour. Check it every 15 minutes, and add water or more broth if it is dry-looking. Test the gizzards for done-ness with a table fork; they should be soft.

Change-around: Brown ½ pound of chicken livers in the pan with 1 more Tablespoon margarine. Add them to the casserole about 10 minutes before you are going to take it from the oven.

Lumber Camp Stew

(4 servings)

When the lumberjacks of the Old Northwest came back to camp after a hard day of chopping down trees, the camp cook served them big buckets of this good stew. The woodsmen gobbled it down and mopped up the juice with the cook's home-baked sourdough bread. You could use chunks of unsliced rye for your mop.

1½ pounds stew beef, cut in cubes

1 onion

2 Tablespoons or more corn oil margarine

1½ Tablespoons maple syrup

2 Tablespoons toasted wheat germ

2 tomatoes, or ½ can of tomatoes

2 green peppers

1 bay leaf

1 pinch of thyme

1½ teaspoons salt

1 cup stock or consomme

4 cups water

2 teaspoons salt

6 large or 12 baby carrots

3 large potatoes

1 large onion (the second onion in the recipe)

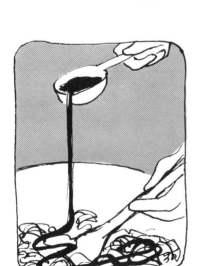

Cut off any big chunks of fat from the meat. Peel 1 onion and slice it. Cook it in margarine in a heavy pot over medium heat until it is yellow.

Cook the meat in the pan until it is brownish, turning to brown all sides. Use more margarine if necessary. Then drizzle the syrup over it. Sprinkle the meat with 1 Tablespoon of wheat germ, turn it over and sprinkle it with the other Tablespoon of wheat germ.

Cook in the pan for 5 more minutes, stirring every minute or two.

Wash the tomatoes and green peppers. Cut each tomato into 4 pieces. Cut each green pepper into 6 or 8 pieces. Clean out the seeds and inside sections. Add them: the tomatoes, the bay leaf, thyme, salt and stock or consomme to the meat in the pot. Cover, turn the heat to very low, and let it cook for about 2 hours.

While the meat is cooking, scrub the carrots and peel the potatoes. Cut the carrots into 3-inch pieces.

Cut the potatoes into 2 or 3 pieces each. Peel the second onion and cut it in half.

When the meat has cooked for 1 hour, put these vegetables into the stew. Let them cook until they feel soft when you stick a table fork into them. This will take another hour.

Test the meat with a fork, too. When it is cooked, serve the stew.

What Else? Something crisp, like a green salad.

Liver Bobs

(4 servings)

We've done it! We've found a liver dish that even someone who's always turned up his nose at this important food will just *have* to like!

> 1 pound calf or baby beef liver (fresh, not frozen, if possible)
> ¼ pound sliced boiled or baked ham
> 3 medium-sized tomatoes, slightly under-ripe
> ¼ cup corn oil
> 1 teaspoon salt
> ¼ teaspoon pepper
> juice of ½ lemon

Turn the broiler on, or build a fire in your charcoal grill.

Cut off any skin or hard skin-like bits from the liver. Then cut it into strips about 3 inches long and 1 inch wide.

Cut the ham into pieces about the same size. Wash the tomatoes and cut into eighths.

String the 2 meats and the tomatoes on 4 long skewers: liver, ham, tomato, liver, ham, tomato, etc. Fold the meat if that's easier.

Mix the oil, lemon juice, salt and pepper. With a pastry brush, brush this on the skewered food.

Put the skewers under the broiler or on the grill, about 4 inches from the heat. Broil for 3 minutes. Turn so that the other side of the meat is toward the heat. Broil 3 minutes more.

What Else? Serve over brown rice.

Farm Chicken

(4 servings)

A busy farm cook can start this dish, do the first part, and then go out and help milk the cows. After the milking, the cook can finish the chicken.

    1 onion
    1 broiling or frying chicken, cut in pieces
    2 teaspoons salt
    2 cups water
    2 Tablespoons corn oil
    salt and pepper
    dried minced garlic

Peel the onion and cut it in half. Put it and the chicken in a large pot with a lid, add 2 cups of cold water and 2 teaspoons salt. Cover the pot, put it over medium heat. When steam puffs out, lower the heat and cook for about 20 minutes.

Light the oven and set it for 400°. Lay the chicken pieces side by side in a baking dish. Pour the cooking water over them.

Measure the oil into a cup and drizzle it over the chicken. Sprinkle the pieces with salt and pepper, and, if you like it, a little dried minced garlic. Bake it for 20 minutes. If it's not nicely browned by then, leave it in longer, checking it every 5 minutes.

When it's ready, put it on a platter and pour some of the juice over it.

What Else? You could bake zucchini squash while the chicken is in the oven.

Oven "Fried" Chicken

(4 servings)

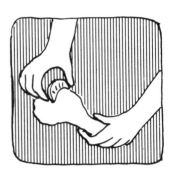

Real fried chicken is delicious, but we get a lot more fat from it than we need or can use. This tastes very much like it, but there's no fat for the chicken to soak up.

> 1 frying chicken, cut in pieces
> ¼ lemon
> 1 cup toasted wheat germ
> 1 teaspoon salt
> ¼ teaspoon basil, tarragon or marjoram
> 1 egg
> ¼ cup milk
> 1 Tablespoon corn oil

Rub the chicken pieces with a piece of lemon. Choose an herb, and rub it into the chicken.

Put the wheat germ and salt into a flat soup bowl. In another soup bowl mix the egg, milk and oil with a fork.

Set the oven for 325°. Grease a baking pan or cookie sheet with a little corn oil margarine. Dip the chicken pieces in the egg mixture and then in the wheat germ. Put them on the pan.

Bake the chicken for 45 minutes. Stick a fork in the meaty part of the leg. Take it out. If the juice that runs out is pink, cook the chicken longer. It is done when the juice that runs out has no color.

Fish Fingers

(4 servings)

1 pound filet of flounder or sole
½ cup toasted wheat germ
¼ cup sesame seeds
1 teaspoon salt
½ teaspoon paprika
1 large egg or 2 small ones
2 Tablespoons corn oil
1 lemon
corn oil margarine to grease the pan

Grease a flat baking pan with margarine. Set the oven for 350°.

Lay the fish pieces out and cut them into strips about 1 inch wide and 4 inches long.

Put the wheat germ and sesame seed into a flat soup bowl with the salt and paprika. Break the egg into another flat bowl. Add the corn oil. Beat it with a fork to mix it.

Roll each piece of fish in the wheat germ mixture, then in the egg mixture, then in the wheat germ again. Lay them on the baking pan as you coat them. This is the same way you coated the chicken in the last recipe, except that there's an extra layer of the wheat germ.

Bake the fish for 15 minutes.

Use a pancake turner to move it from the pan to a platter. Cut the lemon in 4 and serve it with the fish.

Sea Surprise

(4 servings)

½ medium-sized onion
1 large or 2 small carrots
1 pound filet of flounder or sole
1 tomato
8 ounces (1 container) plain yogurt
corn oil margarine
salt and paprika

Peel the onion and slice it very thin. Scrape the carrot and slice it into thin rounds. Put these vegetables into a small pan with just enough water to cover them and ¼ teaspoon salt. Bring the water to boiling over medium heat, turn down the heat so the water just bubbles slowly, and cook until almost all the water is gone.

Light the oven and set it for 350°.

Tear off 4 pieces of aluminum foil, each about 10 inches long. Grease 1 side of each with margarine.

Divide the fish into 4 portions, and put 1 portion on one half of each piece of foil. You are going to fold the foil over to cover the fish, that's why you just put it on one half.

Wash the tomato and slice it with a sharp knife into 4 thick slices. Put 1 slice on each portion of fish. Use a slotted spoon to divide the cooked vegetables evenly over the fish. Finally, top each with 2 Tablespoons of yogurt and a sprinkle of salt and paprika.

Fold the foil over the fish, and fold each open edge over 2 or 3 times so that you have leak-proof packages. Bake them in a baking dish, in case they aren't *quite* leakproof!

Bake the fish for 15 minutes. Give each diner a package and let him open it himself.

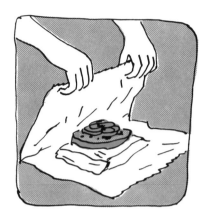

What Else? Whole wheat biscuits, baked before the fish goes in the oven, kept warm just sitting on top of the stove where the oven warms them.

Change-around: Use slices of green pepper instead of the carrots, or with them. Put some peas on the fish, too. Center a mushroom cap on the tomato slice. Or for a very special surprise, put 2 or 3 shelled shrimp on each portion of fish.

Pizza

(one 14″ pizza)

There are some places where you just *have* to have white flour, and pizza dough is one. So we used the famous Cornell triple-rich, white bread recipe.

1½ cups warm water
1 envelope active dry yeast
1 Tablespoon honey
3 cups *unbleached* white flour, or more
1½ Tablespoons toasted wheat germ
¼ teaspoon pepper
¼ cup full-fat soy flour*
½ cup powdered skim milk
2 teaspoons salt
1 Tablespoon corn or olive oil

Mix the water, yeast and honey. Let it stand while you measure and sift the flour, wheat germ, soy flour and skim milk powder. Stir the yeast mixture, adding the salt, pepper, and 1½ cups of the flour. With an electric mixer, beat it 2 minutes (or 75 strokes with a spoon).

Add the oil and 1½ more cups flour. Mix with your hands. If the dough is sticky, add a handful of flour and mix it in. Do this until the dough is still soft but no longer sticky.

Oil a 14-inch pizza pan or 2 large pie plates.

Grease a bowl, put in the dough, and turn it so it gets an overall coating of shortening. Cover with a towel and set it on the top shelf of your oven. If there is no gas pilot light, put a big bowl of very hot water on the lower shelf.

When the dough has risen to twice its size,

punch it down, gather it into a ball and pat and stretch it out to fit the pan or pans.

Light the oven and set it for 350°.

½ pound skim milk mozzarella cheese

1 6-ounce can tomato sauce

½ 6-ounce can tomato paste

½ teaspoon dried oregano

1 small clove garlic or ¼ teaspoon dried garlic

½ teaspoon salt

grated Parmesan or Romano cheese (or both)

1 Tablespoon corn or olive oil

¼ teaspoon pepper

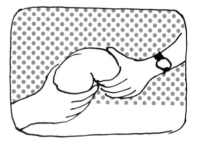

In a small bowl, mix the tomato sauce and the tomato paste, the oregano, crumbled between your fingers, and the garlic, peeled and cut very small or put through a garlic press. Add the salt and pepper. Mix all together well.

Grate the cheese or cut it into small squares. Spread half the tomato mixture over the dough, sprinkle the mozzarella on top, then add the rest of the sauce. Shake grated cheese over it all and sprinkle the oil on the top.

Bake the pizza for about 30 minutes, or until the crust is brown and the cheese melted.

Change-around: Add whatever you like to the sauce—salami, anchovies, mushrooms, etc.

CHAPTER 4

Good Green Growing Things

Wonderful complicated chemical happenings go on all the time in our bodies. The minerals and vitamins that we eat control these happenings, and keep them working the way they should.

We get most of our vitamins and minerals from fruits and vegetables; different growing things give us different hidden treasures. That's why we eat all kinds of fruits and vegetables—not just one or two.

Another reason, of course, is that they taste so good. Here are some ways to serve raw or cooked vegetables that everyone will like. We've kept the fruits for the chapter on desserts and sweets, because they really are that.

All-Green Salad (for four)

1 big head of Boston lettuce, 1 medium head of romaine, OR 1 small bunch of escarole, OR 2 heads of Bibb lettuce, OR 1 pound of spinach leaves OR any combination of greens

½ small clove of garlic

1 teaspoon salt (sea salt* or kosher salt is good here)

½ cup corn or olive oil

2 Tablespoons vinegar or lemon juice

½ teaspoon black pepper (ground, if possible, in a pepper mill)

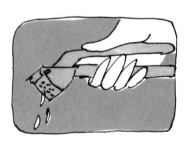

Wash the greens well in cold water, and shake them dry or dry them in a dishtowel.

Peel the garlic and crush it in a garlic press or chop it into *very* small pieces. Put it in a salad bowl with the salt. Rub them together with the back of a wooden spoon. Add the oil. Stir it well. Then add the vinegar or lemon juice and pepper.

Tear the greens with your hands into bite-sized pieces and put them in the bowl. Toss the salad with 2 big spoons or salad servers. Pick some of it up from the bottom, drop it on top, keep doing this until the dressing coats it all.

> Change-around: Add vegetables—celery, green pepper, cauliflower florets, anything you like. Try some black or green olives; they make your salad very fancy!

"Thing" Salads

Salads that look like something else are fun for parties, or when you have a friend over for lunch or supper.

Ladybugs

4 medium-sized tomatoes
6 pitted black olives OR
6 red radishes
Lettuce, escarole or romaine

Wash the tomatoes, the lettuce, and the radishes if you're using them. Shake the lettuce dry and put some fresh-looking green leaves on each of 4 plates.

Clean the radishes—cut off the roots and leaves. Cut 4 of them, or the 4 black olives, into little bits for the ladybug's spots.

Cut the tomatoes in two, cutting from the stem end to the bottom. Then cut each half across. Arrange them in pairs to make a ladybug's body. Put 2 ladybugs on each plate, on a bed of green. Add spots to each one and put a half olive or radish at the top of each for her head.

Salad Flowers

You can make all sorts of flowers from fruits and vegetables.

Pile up a small heap of green pepper slivers or of chopped cooked beets. Set orange or tangerine sections around it. Make stems and leaves of green pepper.

Make carrot curls by running a scraper along a washed, peeled carrot and rolling up the strips. These are good chrysanthemum petals. Use celery stalks split down the middle or green pepper strips for stems.

Parsley makes stems and leaves of flowers whose heads are rounds of raw carrot. Put a whole little field of them on each salad plate.

Make up some salad flowers of your own with vegetables and fruits.

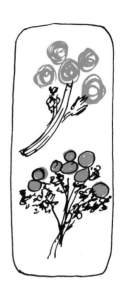

Sailboats

(4 servings)

1 small cantaloupe
2 square slices of cheese: American, Swiss, Muenster—anything so long as it's square
lettuce or other greens
You'll need some toothpicks, too

Wash the lettuce and shake it dry. Gather it into a bunch, cut it into strips, and put a handful on each of 4 plates. This is the lake, or possibly the ocean. (Choppy today, isn't it?)

Clean the seeds from the cantaloupe and cut it into 4 pieces, cutting from one end to the other, so that the pieces are shaped like crescents. Stand them up; if they won't stand, cut a little bit off the bottom of each to make a flat place.

Cut each slice of cheese in half diagonally. Using toothpicks, stick a triangle of cheese into each cantaloupe boat like a sail. Set the boats on the green waves.

The Old Apple Tree (4 servings)

½ pound raw spinach
1 pint cherry tomatoes
4 pieces of celery, each about 3 inches long
salt
juice of 1 lemon

Wash the spinach well in cold water and shake it dry. Bunch it together and cut it into small pieces with a knife or kitchen shears.

Wash the celery stalks and the tomatoes.

On each of 4 plates, put a stalk of celery for the tree trunk, a big bunch of spinach for the leaves. Dot the little tomatoes around on the spinach for apples. Sprinkle salt over it all, and a squeeze of lemon.

Cut-Out Salads

Use cookie cutters on thick slices of cooked beets, slices of melon, or other vegetables, fruits and cheeses. Put the shapes on a bed of greens.

Make up some "Thing" salads of your own. Use fruits, vegetables, cheese, hard-cooked eggs, cold meat and fish—whatever goes well in salads.

Cole Slaw

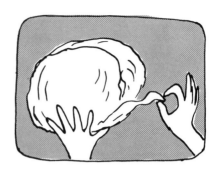

(4 servings)

½ head of cabbage
1 carrot
1 small onion
½ green pepper
½ cup mayonnaise
1 teaspoon lemon juice
1 teaspoon honey

Rinse the cabbage, take off any wilted outside leaves, and shred it with a sharp knife or grate it on the grater. The solid part in the middle is a little too tough for salad.

Wash the carrot, peel the onion, wash the green pepper. With the scraper, make carrot strips and add them to the cabbage in a big bowl. Slice the onion into thin slices, separate them into rings, and add to the salad. Cut the green pepper into strips, cut the strips into bits, put them in, too.

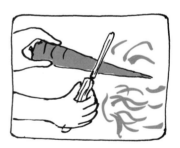

Mix the mayonnaise with the lemon juice and honey; add it to the vegetables, and mix very well.

Change-arounds: You can make the same dressing as in "All Green Salad" instead of mayonnaise.

OR Sprinkle celery seed over the salad and mix it in.

Raw Vegetable Dip

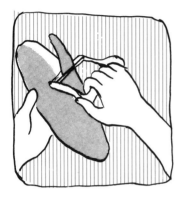

Use any sort of raw vegetables: carrots, green peppers, scallions, turnips, Brussels sprouts, mushrooms, cucumbers, radishes, cauliflower, squash, whatever looks good in the market. There is almost no vegetable that can't be eaten raw—although some taste better than others that way!

You also need:
   ½ cup cottage cheese
   ½ cup plain yogurt
   ¼ onion (start with a whole one)
   1 teaspoon celery salt

Wash the vegetables. Peel the ones that need peeling, trim the ones that need trimming. Cut them into pieces that are easy to pick up. Divide the cauliflower into little flowers.

In a bowl mix the cheese, yogurt and celery salt. Peel the onion and grate about ¼ of it into the mixture. Put the bowl in the middle of a platter and arrange the vegetables around it.

Change-arounds: If you like hot things, add ½ teaspoon of horseradish or 3 shakes of Tabasco sauce to the dip.
Shake some paprika on the top for color.

Sunny String Beans

(4 servings)

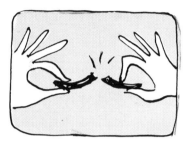

Once I rode in a bus next to an elderly man who spent the whole trip cleaning the green beans in a bag on his lap. I hope he cooked them with a tiny bit of water, because it keeps in the flavor and the vitamins and minerals too.

Choose a pot with a heavy bottom and a tight-fitting lid.

> 1 pound string beans. Young tender ones are best.
> 1½ Tablespoons corn oil margarine
> 1½ Tablespoons butter
> 1/3 cup water or meat stock
> salt and pepper
> ½ cup hulled sunflower seeds

Run cold water over the beans, snap off their ends and break them in half. If there is a thread, pull it off as far as it will pull.

Put them in a saucepan with the liquid. Cover the pan tightly and cook over the lowest heat possible for 15 minutes.

Put the butter, margarine and sunflower seeds in a pan, over medium heat. Mix until the fat is melted and the seeds slightly toasted.

Take the cover off the bean pot, let whatever water is left evaporate, add the butter mixture and salt and pepper.

Change-around: Substitute for the seeds ½ cup slivered almonds, toasted, or pieces of pecan or walnut. Then they will be "*Nutty String Beans!*"

Wrapped Peas

(4 servings)

Cooking peas this way means that there's no water to dissolve out the vitamins and minerals. The flavor stays in, too.

4–8 big leaves of lettuce

2 pounds fresh peas in the pod OR

2 10-ounce packages frozen peas

2 Tablespoons corn oil margarine

½ teaspoon dried herb. (Try mint, rosemary or thyme.)

1 teaspoon salt

¼ teaspoon pepper

Shell the peas if they are fresh. Wash the lettuce. Put half the leaves on the bottom of a 2-quart or larger saucepan with a lid.

Add the peas, margarine, the herb, crumbled in your hand first, the salt and pepper. Put the rest of the lettuce over the top of all this. Cover the pot and put it over medium heat.

When the lid feels hot to your touch, turn the heat to low. Cook the peas 17 minutes from this point.

Your 17 minutes are up! Take out the lettuce. (I eat it in the kitchen while I'm getting ready to serve the peas!) Serve the peas.

Baked Zucchini (4 servings)

There's a time in late summer when it seems that every vegetable counter is loaded with this good squash, from tiny to enormous. Cook some this easy way.

> 2 pounds zucchini (smaller ones are better)
> 1 large can tomato sauce
> ½ cup grated cheese
> salt, pepper, oregano

Set the oven for 350° and spread a little corn oil margarine in a casserole.

Wash the zucchini under cold water. Without peeling it, slice it into thin rounds. Put a layer of these rounds in the casserole. Sprinkle it with salt and pepper. Add another layer, season it, and keep on until all the squash is in.

In a bowl, mix the tomato sauce with 1 teaspoon dried oregano, which you crumble in your hand first.

Pour the sauce over the zucchini. Sprinkle the grated cheese over the top. Cover the casserole.

Bake it until the zucchini is soft—about 25 minutes.

Country Carrots (4 servings)

For those who like sweet carrots . . .

> 6 large carrots
> 1 Tablespoon brown sugar
> 2 Tablespoons corn oil margarine
> ½ cup orange juice
> a few shakes of salt

Scrub the carrots and cut into little rounds, as thin as dimes—or anyhow quarters.

Put the orange juice and carrots into a saucepan over medium heat and, when the orange juice boils, turn the heat to very low, cover the pan, and let the carrots cook for half an hour. Look at them every 5 minutes or so; if the orange juice looks almost gone, add a little water—about ¼ cup at a time.

After 30 minutes, test the carrots with a fork. If they are soft, add the sugar, margarine and salt, and cook with the cover off until all the liquid is gone and the sugar and margarine have coated the carrots.

Change-around: For those who *don't* like sweet carrots . . . cook them with water, a dash of salt, and ½ teaspoon celery seed. Put margarine on them when they are done.

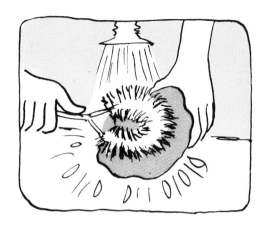 

Baked Potatoes (4 servings)

Set the oven for 375°.

Scrub 4 big potatoes with cold water and a brush. Prick them in several places with a fork. Put them in the oven; depending on their size they will take from 45 minutes to 1½ hours to bake.

Test them for doneness by sticking a table fork into the largest one. If it feels soft all the way in, the potato is ready.

When you take them out, hold each potato in a potholder or towel and squeeze it gently, rolling it around in your fingers. Cut an "X" in the side of each, and serve with a dollop of butter or margarine, or some plain yogurt, and salt.

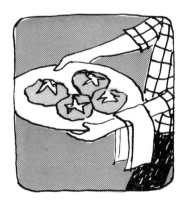

There are aluminum spikes that you stick into the raw potato. By carrying heat to the center, they speed up the baking. If you have these and use them, test the potatoes in about 25 minutes.

CHAPTER 5

Time For Something Sweet

Candy and other ordinary sweets made with refined sugar dull your appetite for other food without giving you very much of the nutrition your body needs.

But everybody likes sweets!

In this chapter you'll find some of the many good things you can make with honey, brown sugar, or naturally sweet fresh and dried fruits. After you try them, you may be surprised to find you're eating fewer candy bars and drinking less soda.

Apricot Leather

You need a food grinder for this. I hope you have one, because it's *very* good. It makes a fine snack when you want something sweet and tangy, and a nice, unusual little present all rolled up and tied with a ribbon.

> 1 cup dried apricots (unsulfured, if possible)

Rinse the apricots. Set up the food grinder with the finest blade—the one with no holes at all. Put the apricots through twice.

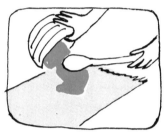

Spread out a square of plastic wrap or waxed paper, and put half the ground apricots on it. Cover them with another square of wrap or paper, and roll them with a rolling pin until they make a very thin, flat sheet. If the paper breaks while you are working, just put another piece on top of it so the fruit won't stick to the rolling pin. Turn the whole thing over often; that will keep the wrap or paper from wrinkling too much.

Repeat this with the other half of the apricots on more plastic wrap or paper.

To eat the "leather," peel it from the paper.

Change-arounds: Use dried peaches or pears with the apricots, or instead of them.

OR Add ½ cup ground raisins to the apricots and mix them well before rolling. This makes a delicious, if rather sticky, mixture.

Honey Nut Ice Cream

(this makes 2 ice-cube trayfuls)

1 Tablespoon (1 envelope) unflavored gelatin
¼ cup water
2 cups milk or light cream
½ cup honey
1 cup evaporated milk (don't add water!)
3 teaspoons vanilla
¼ cup shelled nuts—walnuts, almonds or pecans

Put the gelatin in a cup and pour the water over it.

Heat 1 cup of milk until it feels hot, when you put a drop on your hand, but is not boiling. Take it from the heat and add the gelatin. Stir until it melts.

Add the honey and stir it in. Honey is a little bit acid and could cause the milk to "curdle," or separate into little lumps. This looks funny, but won't change the taste. Beat it hard with a fork or beater and go on with the recipe.

Add the rest of the milk, the evaporated milk, and the vanilla.

Mix it all well and pour it into 2 ice-cube trays. Set the refrigerator at the coldest point, and let the mixture freeze to a mush. This takes about an hour, depending on how your own refrigerator works.

When the cream is mushy, take it out, dump it into a big bowl, and beat it with an electric mixer or rotary eggbeater until it is soft and fluffy. Add the nuts, stir them in gently. Put the mixture back in the trays and let it freeze to ice cream!

> Change-around: Leave out the vanilla. When you take the ice cream from the freezer to beat it, add 4 mashed bananas and 2 Tablespoons lemon juice.

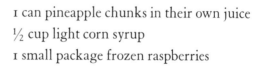

Garden Sundae Topping

(makes 4 sundaes)

1 can pineapple chunks in their own juice
½ cup light corn syrup
1 small package frozen raspberries

Let the raspberries thaw partly—about 1 hour. Open the package, and measure ¼ cup of the juice. Put it in a small saucepan with ¼ cup of the juice from the pineapple. Add the corn syrup, and mix.

Set the pan over low heat. When the liquid boils, turn the heat down so it simmers, and keep it cooking for 5 minutes.

Drain off the rest of the juice from both kinds of fruit and save it for another dessert. Add the fruit to the syrup in the pan, let it cool, and spoon it over ice cream.

 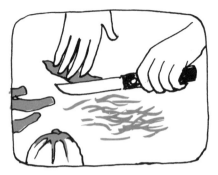

Orange Glory

(4 servings)

4 oranges
juice of 1 lemon
2 Tablespoons honey

Wash 1 orange and cut thin strips of peel from it with a vegetable scraper. Use a knife to cut these strips into little bits the size of toothpicks. Put these in a small saucepan.

Peel all the oranges and cut them into round slices. Do this on a plate. Pour the juice that runs out into the saucepan, but put the slices in a bowl.

Cut the lemon in half and squeeze the juice from it; add this to the pan. Add the honey to the juices and peel.

Bring the mixture to a boil on medium heat. Let it bubble slowly—turn the heat down—for 5 minutes. Then pour it over the orange slices.

Chill the dish in the refrigerator for an hour or more.

Change-around: Sprinkle the oranges with 3 Tablespoons of grated unsweetened* coconut before serving them.

Jumble Jell (4 servings)

2 cups grape juice, unsweetened
1 envelope plain gelatin
1 small can Bing cherries
½ cup shelled walnuts, broken into halves

Put ¼ cup grape juice in a small bowl or cup and sprinkle the gelatin over it. Heat the rest of the juice in a small saucepan. When it is hot, take it from the heat, add the gelatin mixture, and stir until the gelatin melts.

Pour the juice into a dish and set it in the refrigerator for 3 hours or overnight. When it is stiff, drain the cherries, put them and the nuts in the dish with the gelatin, and stir them in.

Change-arounds: You can use different juices and different fruits (any except fresh or frozen pineapple). Clear juices make a nicer gel than cloudy ones. They're all best unsweetened.

 # Baked Apples (4 servings)

4 large McIntosh, Cortland, Rome or other
  apples
½ cup dried currants
½ cup brown sugar
1 teaspoon cinnamon
4 shakes nutmeg
½ cup water or more

Light the oven and set it for 350°.

Wash the apples. Take out the stems and with a corer or a knife, dig out the core from the other end. Try to leave some apple below the core, at the stem end. Peel a wide strip of skin off the end that you cored. Set the apples stem side down in a flat baking pan. Fill the core holes with currants and about 2 teaspoons of brown sugar for each apple. Sprinkle cinnamon over each, shake the nutmeg can over each. Put the rest of the brown sugar on the top of the apples.

Pour the water gently over each apple. There should be some at the bottom of the pan.

Bake the apples, basting them every 10 minutes with the pan liquid. They are done when they have burst out of their skins and are very soft. It takes half to three-quarters of an hour, depending on the kind of apple.

Serve warm or cold with the juice from the pan, and milk or plain yogurt.

After The Waltz

(4 servings)

A Joyful Dessert From Vienna
(and a good use for leftover
dark bread crumbs!)

1 cup of dark pumpernickel or rye crumbs
(make them in the blender, or toast slices
of bread and crush them in a plastic bag
with a rolling pin)
2 cups applesauce, bought or homemade
½ cup raisins
¼ cup chopped nuts (see page 93)
1 shake of cinnamon
1 egg
margarine for greasing a casserole

Set the oven for 350°. Grease a casserole that holds at least 1½ quarts.

Mix everything together but the egg. Put the mixture into the casserole.

Beat the egg until it is frothy. Pour it over the applesauce mixture.

Bake 35 minutes. Serve hot or cold. If you like, pour milk over each serving or top with a glob of plain yogurt, or yogurt mixed with honey.

Stuffed Prunes

Prunes. Pitted, or slit them down 1 side and pull out the pits.

Large pieces of walnuts or pecans, or whole almonds.

Honey, unsweetened coconut*, and sesame seeds for rolling.

Put a nutmeat inside each prune. Roll in honey and then in coconut or sesame seeds.

Israeli Poppyseed Candy

1 cup poppy seeds
1 cup honey
½ cup nuts

Run cold water through the poppy seeds in a fine strainer and let drain. Chop the nuts.

Put the seeds in a saucepan with the honey and nuts, and bring to a boil over medium heat. Boil 8 minutes; if mixture starts browning sooner, take it off.

Spread on a board or plate and cut into squares while still hot. It will be chewy when cool.

Fruit And Nut Balls

1 cup dried fruit (apricots, prunes or other)
1/3 cup nuts (see page 93)
2 Tablespoons water
½ cup unsweetened* coconut
More coconut* for rolling the balls in

Cut up the fruit into very little pieces. Cut the nuts, and let them crumble as you cut.

Mix everything but the coconut. Roll into little balls and roll each ball in coconut.

Banana Freeze

4 ripe but firm bananas
juice of 1 lemon
coconut* or sesame seeds for rolling

Peel bananas. Cut in half around the middle, and use a pastry brush to paint them with lemon juice. Roll in coconut or sesame seeds. Wrap each one in plastic wrap, foil, or waxed paper and freeze.

There's a different taste to bananas if they have been frozen in the refrigerator freezer or in the deep freeze. Try them both ways if you can.

Snacks For Snatching

Keep on a handy table, for munching, a mixture of:

Peanuts
Raisins
Sunflower seeds (hulled)
Pumpkin seeds (hulled)
Roasted soybeans
Pine nuts ("pignoli")
Shredded unsweetened coconut*

Keep in the refrigerator, ready to snatch, a bowl of raw vegetables, cleaned and cut into convenient pieces, covered with plastic wrap so they can be seen and remembered. Add olives of different kinds, pickles, bits of cheese.

79

CHAPTER 6

LONG LIVE THE BAKER!

Baking Day

In some ways, the most satisfying kind of cooking is baking. You put dough in the oven and out come cakes, cookies, breads . . . a magic change!

The "bakings" we give you here are made with whole grain flours. A look at this grain of wheat shows why. It's drawn as though we could see through the outside skin. This is what's in it:

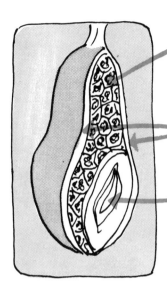

ENDOSPERM: has sugar, starch, and cellulose, which is not a food but helps food move through our bodies.

BRAN: has protein, iron, other minerals, and the whole family of B vitamins.

GERM: has protein, minerals, vitamins and fat. (This is called the "germ" because it is the heart of the wheat. It has nothing to do with the "germs" that cause disease.)

Every grain, or "berry," of wheat has these three parts. You can see where most of the food value is—in the *bran* and in the *germ*. Yet when wheat is milled for everyday white flour, these parts are taken out! Only the endosperm—the starch and sugar and "roughage"—are left!

So the miller then "enriches" the white flour; he adds manufactured vitamins and iron to it. But the natural vitamins are gone, and so is the protein and many of the other minerals.

That's why the recipes here use whole grain flour. They have more flavor, too. Wait until you make these cakes and cookies! You'll even find directions for baking real yeast bread. You'll like the smell of it baking . . . and the taste even more!

Graham Cake

(a luscious cake for a birthday . . . or an un-birthday!)

I was very suspicious and pessimistic before I tried this. How could a *whole wheat* cake taste *really* like a cake? Well, it does—and better than most. Bake it and see!

> 2 cups graham* (whole wheat pastry) flour
> 2½ teaspoons baking powder
> 1 cup egg whites (About 8 eggs. Save the yolks for custards and omelets.)
> 1 cup buttermilk
> 2 teaspoons vanilla
> 1½ cups brown sugar, packed tight to measure
> 1/3 cup (2/3 stick) corn oil margarine
> flour and margarine for the pans

Grease two 8- or 9-inch round or square cake pans with margarine and shake a little flour around in each. Dump out the flour that doesn't stick.

Set the oven for 325°.

Measure the flour into a bowl and add the baking powder. Separate the eggs. (See page 92.)

Using an eggbeater or your electric mixer, beat the egg whites until they are nice and stiff.

Put the buttermilk, vanilla, sugar and margarine into your blender. Turn it on for 1 minute,

or until it is all mixed together. OR blend these ingredients with an electric beater.

Stir this mixture into the flour.

Fold in the egg whites. (See page 93.) Divide the batter into the pans and bake the layers for 25 minutes. Check them: if the cake looks done, press it gently in the middle with your finger. If it springs back, it is done. If not, give it more time.

Take the pans from the oven. Let them cool slightly, then turn them upside down and tap gently. Cool the cake completely before icing it.

All Those Egg Yolks!

There are so many ways to use up egg yolks that you won't mind having these left over *or* the 2 more from the icing on the next page. Add them to a whole egg for scrambling, use them instead of whole eggs in Egg Drop Soup, make cup custards with them. There are many cake and cookie recipes that use just egg yolks. They'll keep in the refrigerator, covered with water, for several days.

Icing For Graham Cake

1 cup brown sugar

¼ cup water

2 egg whites

1 teaspoon vanilla

¼ teaspoon cream of tartar

1 shake of salt

Stir the sugar and water in a saucepan over medium heat until the sugar melts. If you have a candy thermometer, clip it to the pot and cook till the temperature reaches 275°. Otherwise, test the syrup by dropping a little from a spoon; it should leave firm, but not hard, threads hanging.

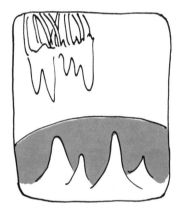

Meanwhile, separate the eggs (see page 92). Save the yolks for another recipe. Add the cream of tartar, salt and vanilla to the whites. Beat them with a rotary beater or electric mixer until they are stiff.

Pour the sugar mixture into the egg whites, beating them as you do. (You'll need either an electric beater or a helper for this.) Beat for a minute or two after all the sugar is in.

Spread on the cake.

Date Bars

(about 22 bars)

¾ cup nuts (see page 93)

½ cup pitted dates (you can buy them pitted)

½ cup graham* or regular whole wheat flour

3 eggs

1 cup brown sugar, packed tight to measure

½ teaspoon baking powder

a pinch of salt

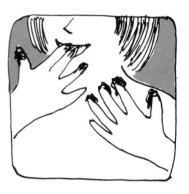

Set the oven for 350°. Grease an 8- or 9-inch square pan, or an 11 x 7-inch cake pan. Line it with waxed paper, and grease the paper.

Put 2 Tablespoons of the flour into a cup. Cut the dates into small bits. As you do each one, roll the bits in flour so they won't stick. Put the dates into a bowl. Cut the nuts into small pieces and add to the dates.

In another bowl, beat the eggs with a beater and add the sugar, a little at a time. Beat 2 minutes after all the sugar is in.

Add the rest of the flour, the baking powder, and salt. Stir until it is well mixed. Stir in the dates and nuts.

Spread in the pan and put in the oven. Check after 20 minutes. It is done when the center will spring back when you press it gently.

Cool slightly, cut into bars, and take them from the pan with a spatula.

Banana Loaf

An easy-to-make, delicious tea loaf—good for snacks or dessert.

> 1½ cups whole wheat or graham* flour
> 2 teaspoons baking powder
> ½ teaspoon baking soda
> ½ teaspoon salt
> ¼ cup corn oil margarine (½ stick)
> ½ cup brown sugar
> 1 egg
> 1 teaspoon vanilla
> 2 very ripe (but not brown) bananas
> 1¼ cups bran flakes (cereal)
> ½ cup nuts (see page 93.)

Set the oven for 350°. Grease a loaf pan.

Sift together the flour, baking powder, soda and salt.

In another bowl or a blender, mix the egg, vanilla, margarine, sugar and cut-up bananas. Blend or beat them with an electric beater or a wooden spoon. You might have to stop a blender and push the ingredients down a few times. If you use a spoon, mash the bananas first. Add the bran and nuts. Gradually add the flour mixture, stirring just until it's mixed.

Put the batter in the loaf pan and smooth it down evenly. Bake for 45 minutes to 1 hour. It is done when it is nicely browned and springs back when you press it gently. Let it cool in the pan. Slice it when cool.

Jeannie's Bannocks (8 wedges)

A Scottish quick bread very much like scones, good with fried chicken or barbecued ribs or roast beef or . . . almost anything!

1 cup cornmeal

1 cup quick-cooking (but not "instant") oats

1 teaspoon baking soda

½ teaspoon salt

2 Tablespoons maple syrup

½ cup buttermilk

2 Tablespoons corn or peanut oil

½ teaspoon ginger

Set the oven for 350°.

Mix the cornmeal, baking soda, salt and oatmeal. Add the syrup and stir. Mix the milk and oil, and add it to the dry mixture. Add the ginger.

Work the dough with your hands. It will be crumbly at first, but as you squeeze it, it will become more like dough, and will stick so you can knead it. Knead it for 3 to 5 minutes.

Grease a cookie sheet. Roll half the dough into a ball and flatten it on the sheet with your hand into a round. If the edge is raggedy, smooth it with your fingers. Cut the round in 4 and separate the quarters a little.

Do the same with the other half of the dough.

Bake for 20 to 30 minutes. Take it out when it is firm and just beginning to brown. Serve the bannocks with butter.

Oatmeal Cookies

(about 60 cookies)

¾ cup corn oil margarine

1½ cups brown sugar, packed tight

1 egg

¼ cup water

1 teaspoon vanilla

1 cup whole wheat or graham* flour

1 teaspoon salt

½ teaspoon soda

3 cups uncooked quick or old-fashioned oats

¾ cup raisins

3 Tablespoons toasted wheat germ

Grease one or more cookie sheets; set the oven for 350°.

Mix the margarine, sugar, egg, water and vanilla together with an electric mixer, in the blender, or with a wooden spoon, and beat it until it looks well mixed and creamy.

Mix the flour, salt and soda. Add it to the creamed mixture and mix it well. Add the oatmeal and raisins.

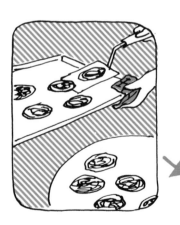

Drop by teaspoonfuls onto the cookie sheet, leaving room for them to spread. Bake 12 to 15 minutes. Check after 10 minutes, again at 12 and 15. When they just begin to brown around the edges, they are done.

Raisin Drop Cookies

2 cups raisins

½ pound (2 sticks) corn oil margarine

1 cup brown sugar, packed tight

3 eggs

½ cup milk

2 cups whole wheat or graham* flour

1½ teaspoons baking powder

½ teaspoon salt

½ teaspoon cinnamon

½ teaspoon nutmeg

¾ cup unsweetened coconut*

2¼ cups bran flakes

Set the oven for 375°. Grease a cookie sheet lightly with corn oil margarine.

Plump the raisins by pouring boiling water over them and letting them stand 5 minutes. Drain.

Meanwhile, mix the eggs, milk, sugar, margarine in a blender, or with an electric beater or a spoon. Beat it until it is nice and creamy.

Add the flour, baking powder, salt, spices, coconut and bran flakes. Then add raisins.

Drop from a teaspoon onto the cookie sheet. Bake for 12 to 15 minutes, or until they start to brown around the edges.

Use a pancake turner or spatula to take them from the cookie sheet and put them on a rack or platter to cool.

Aunt May's Whole Wheat Bread

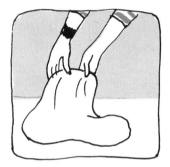

(2 loaves)

4 teaspoons salt

2½ cups lukewarm water

3 Tablespoons unsulfured molasses
   ("Blackstrap"* molasses gives a spicier flavor.)

1 teaspoon active dry yeast

7 cups or more whole wheat flour

5 Tablespoons dry skim milk

corn oil or corn oil margarine for greasing

Measure the flour into a bowl and stir it with a large spoon for 3 minutes.

Mix the salt with 2 cups of water and the molasses in a big bowl. (Grease the measuring spoon before measuring molasses.)

Sprinkle the yeast over ½ cup of water and stir it until it melts. Mix this with the salt and molasses mixture. Then add the flour, stirring it in, and the skim milk powder. Mix it with your hands until it no longer sticks to the bowl. Add more flour, a little at a time, if the dough is sticky.

Now you're ready to knead! ·

Sprinkle flour on a board or clean tabletop. Make the dough into a ball on the board. Flatten it a little and pull the far edge toward you. Press it down and, with the heel of your hand, push it away from you. Turn the dough a quarter turn and do this again. Keep kneading, turning each time, for about 10 minutes. The dough will feel springy and "live."

Wash the bowl and grease it with the oil or margarine. Turn the ball of dough in the bowl so it gets greased all over. Leave it in the bowl, cover it with waxed paper, and put a towel over the top. Set it on the top rack of an unlit oven; put a big pan of hot water on the lower rack. As it cools, change it for hotter water.

The dough should rise until it doubles in size. Test it by sticking two fingers about ¼ inch in. If the holes remain when you take out your hand, it has risen enough. This takes 2 to 3 hours, depending on the yeast, the flour, and the temperature.

Punch the dough down with your fist. Squeeze the edges down to make a ball. Shape it into 2 loaves; put each into a greased loaf pan. Cover the dough again and put it back into the unlit oven to rise until the pans are full —another hour or more.

Put the pans in a warm, draft-free place, and turn the oven on, set for 350°. When it is hot, put in the bread, leaving enough room for air to move around the pans.

Bake for about 1 hour, until the bread looks done. Take it out, turn it out of the pan, and rap on the bottom of the loaf. If it sounds hollow, it is done. If not, put it back in the pan and bake it longer.

A Page of "Hows" and One "What"

How...

...to boil liquid

Put it over medium high heat, and wait for big bubbles to come up from the bottom and break at the surface of the liquid. When this is happening very fast, and the top is bubbly, the water or other liquid is boiling.

When small bubbles come slowly to the top, it is *simmering*.

If you have solid food in the liquid (like rice or noodles) it will rise in the pot. Watch it, and if it gets near the edge turn down the heat. Milk will do this, too.

...to separate eggs

You need 3 different containers: 1 for the yolks, 1 for the whites, and 1 small one to work with. Eggs separate best at room temperature.

Tap an egg around the middle with a sharp knife. Hold it over the small bowl and pull the shell apart with your thumbs, holding the egg vertically. Let the white run into the bowl.

Pour the egg yolk back and forth from one half shell to the other. When most of the white has dropped out, put the yolk into one container. Pour the white into the other.

You use the small bowl because sometimes an egg yolk breaks and mixes with the white.

If that happens, the white won't whip. If you are opening more than one egg, you want to keep each new egg white separate until you are sure it is free of yolk, instead of spoiling the ones you've already separated.

. . . to fold in egg whites

Put about half the beaten egg white on the other mixture. With a rubber spatula, cut down into the bowl and then pull up the spatula so that some of the bottom mixture comes with it. Keep doing this, gently pushing egg white to the bottom, carefully pulling the batter from the bottom over the egg white at the top. Don't work too hard at it; do it easily.

When all the first half is mixed in, repeat with the rest of the egg white.

"Folding in" is the way to mix something that's been whipped and not squash all the air out of it.

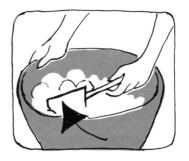

A What...

. . . Nuts

Several recipes call for nuts. You can buy nuts in the shell and remove the shell yourself. You can buy plain shelled nuts. Or you can buy roasted nuts. If you use roasted nuts—peanuts, cashews, mixed nuts—get the kind that says "dry-roasted" on the label, rather than the "regular" kind, roasted with a coating of oil.

The Tools Of Your Trade

Measuring spoons: There are 4 to a set:

1 Tablespoon	½ teaspoon
1 teaspoon	¼ teaspoon

When you measure dry foods, fill the spoon very full. Then, with a table knife, smooth it even at the top. That's called "leveling." All dry ingredients should be measured this way unless the recipe says something different.

Measuring cups: There are 2 kinds. One comes in sets of 4, like the spoons, 1 each for:

1 cup	1/3 cup
½ cup	¼ cup

These are for measuring dry ingredients, like flour or sugar. Level the top as you do with spoons.

The other kind of measuring cup is a single cup with all the measurements marked on it. Use this for liquids. (They level themselves!)

Cooking spoons: Use long-handled spoons for stirring food that is over heat. Use wooden spoons for stirring and the large steel spoons for dipping from one container to another. Large steel spoons with holes in them—"slotted" spoons—let you pick solids out of liquid without getting any liquid.

Pots, pans and kettles: Pots have 2 handles and a lid, and an old-fashioned word for them is

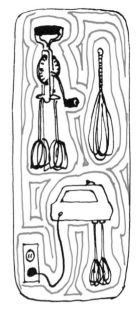

"kettles." Pans are either saucepans, which have one long handle, or frying pans, which are low and flat and also have a long handle. Or it means baking pans, which come in all sizes and shapes and go in the oven.

Eggbeaters: Some are whisks, some are called "rotary" beaters and work mechanically, and some are electric.

Strainers: It is good to have a small one, a large one, and a colander or sieve, which is a kind of overgrown strainer that stands by itself and has fewer holes.

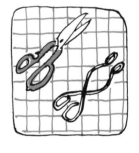

Knives: You need different-sized ones. Always be careful when using a knife. Be sure your other hand isn't in the way. Strangely enough, there's less danger of cutting yourself if the knife is good and sharp. You can control it better.

Kitchen shears are helpful, and so are *tongs* that work like scissors, for picking up small hot things like baked potatoes.

Potholders should be thick. You should have at least 2. Don't use them if they are wet; then the heat will go right through!

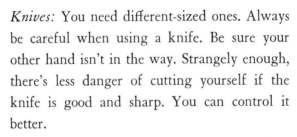

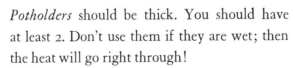

Do you have an *electric blender?* If you do, you will find it very useful for all sorts of things. If not, for some of the recipes in this book, get a jar that holds at least 1 quart (4 measuring cups full), and has a good tight lid that doesn't leak.